A FEW MORE POEMS ON LIFE

By Bill Robertson

CCB Publishing
British Columbia, Canada

Contents

Preface

Since my first book of poetry was published, I continued in my efforts of formulating my thoughts on life in a poetic and rhyming fashion. Having reached my 90s, I have decided to put these remaining poems in this second book. However, unlike the first book, this time the poems are presented in the year in which they were written.

Bill Robertson, May 2020

2014

Friendship Renewed

We met on board a ship at sea,
I was a doctor, so was he.
Fifty-three years ago our careers were on hold,
But both were young, courageous and bold.

Setting out to become an ophthalmic surgeon,
Soli from Mumbai was travelling to London.
On his way home after working in India,
Bill looked forward to being back in old Scotia.

On the voyage to England we both became friends,
But our lives were directing to differing ends.
You to the challenge of Fellowship surgery,
I to the search for financial stability.

We meant to keep contact but it didn't transpire,
As we both were so busy, our lives were on fire.
The years passed so quickly we both did our best,
You back to Mumbai, I went out West.

In my eighty-first year I was thinking one day,
About people I'd known along my life's way.
Of all those in India that I did recall,
My good friend Soli was the best of them all.

In searching around, it caused me some stress,
Till at last in a corner was Soli's address.
It was fifty years old so I wasn't too sure,
But our contact was made and I know 'twill endure.

Bill Robertson 2014

God's Omnipotence

Reproductive seed of all things living
None can exist without My ruling.
Whether moving whether still
All owe everything to My will.

Countless are the actions of My divine power
Ever-changing Endlessness defines Me, hour by hour.
All who bring prosperity, well-being and success
Reflect My ever radiant effulgent prowess.

I am God the Unchanging Everlasting One
Whose Cosmos sustains and permeates everyone.
Man lives in a state of bewildering complexity
I resolve all in Divine Simplicity.

Bill Robertson 2014

The Cosmic Dreamer's God

Divine imaginings appear or disappear
Like fleeting thoughts in a frozen sphere
The fancies of God as Cosmic Dreamer
Stretching out like a holiday streamer.

Tiny bubbles of space-time foam
Creating baby universes looking for a home
When they explode with a mighty clang
It constitutes our world's Big Bang.

As each bubble bursts with enormous force,
Its red hot particles spread out from its source,
And as they cool they create a new world,
Of stars and galaxies they uncurl.

Bill Robertson 2014

Among Vrishnis and Pandavas

In an impersonal way as Spirit he spoke
And realized his incarnation would then invoke
His presence within the Vrishni age
Finding Krishna as a Vasudeva sage.

Among those in the wise Pandava dynasty
Arjuna the ideal disciple is trusty.
Conquering desires, birth, pleasure and pains
Dhananjaya's Divine Treasure attains.

Krishna as Spirit Vyasa outlined
As a muni the Bhagavad Gita defined
The message is clear one must try to be good
Everyday doing whatever one should.

Bill Robertson 2014

Breath of God

Air, the breath of life which God
Sustains all things on Earth that trod
With gentle life-giving prana breeze
Recharging body's feeble knees.

As Rama, Vishnu's incarnation
Vanquishes death, brings liberation
From dire disease it gives release
Blessing all with heavenly peace.

The vehicles of Varuna, god of ocean's seas
Makara devours all the little fishes
Which represent the blazing fires
Of mankind's evil earthly desires.

The Ganges, river blessed by God
As holiest stream on Earth's brown sod
Betokening intuitive wisdom's flow
As would a liberated Yogi bestow.

The taintless sushumna life current of spine
Like thousand-petalled lotus wine
To frontal cortex all demerit
Carries to shores of God's Supreme Spirit.

Bill Robertson 2014

Sestina Number 1

On reaching eighty years one winter's night
I knew I'd still not found that inner peace
For which the search can take a wheen of years
That night a Hindu Swami's wondrous book
Pronounced the age-old need to meditate
And reach communion with the soul of God.

From early youth I'd believed and worshipped God
And said my childish prayers near every night
But never learned the need to meditate
Or found the secret of that inner peace
Though schooled by sermons from the Holy Book
And practised as an Elder over many years.

One thing that troubled me in all these years
Was ministers standing between me and God
There is nothing that says that in all the Holy Book
That's why I decided on that wintry night
To find out if the Swami had found the way to peace
By studying all his writing on how to meditate.

It took two years to learn to meditate.
All the study and tests kept me working hard
Searching out secrets of the way to find peace
Of spiritual communion with God.
The Swami inspired me upon that wintry night
To recommend others should read that special book.

I know that meditation is the way to God
No matter how long or short may be the years
It leads on upwards to the endless light.

Bill Robertson 2014

Winter Humming Bird

The Berwick winter hummingbird
His flits and flashes seem absurd.
From rain-soaked branch or frosty twig
Our feisty friend describes a jig.

Regardless of the rain or snow
With courage facing friend or foe,
Safe beneath his plumage thick
He's perched erect, both strong and quick.

Betimes he flies far wide and high
Returning near where rhodos lie.
Protected 'neath a wooden ledge
They form for him a nectar hedge.

Bill Robertson 2014

Thirty-eighth Anniversary

We've now been married thirty-eight
Happy years in the married state.
With lasting friendship we are blessed,
Which gives us life-long happiness.

Each of us has known tough times,
In different places, different climes.
And of diseases we've had our share,
And braved it all with love and care.

Supporting each the other's intent,
With love and warm encouragement.
We still have dreams we can fulfill,
With special hope we can and will.

Bill Robertson 2014

How Quiet a Life We Lead

There comes a time in every life
When people look for peace.
My wife and I had reached that stage
Regardless of our age.

We searched around both far and near
And soon within a year
We found a corner by the sea
At quite a modest fee.

As days pass swiftly into nights
Some wonder how we live
They little think nor do reflect
How quiet a life we lead.

Rejoicing in our peaceful way
With no one knowing from day to day
How quiet a life we lead.

It is our hope to contemplate
On all the things we've seen
And be prepared to meet our fate
Before the Lord Supreme.

Until that time we'll meditate
To keep our souls serene
And no one will know from day to day
How quiet a life we lead.

Bill Robertson 2014

Gordon and Ruth Curtin

Ruth and Gordon happy twosome
She is lovely, he is handsome.
By their company one is blest,
Soon one knows they are the best.

Gord's special name has Irish lore,
As Ruth's is north-east Scots and more.
Although they seem of different roots,
They're actually in close cahoots.

If Fortune orders that we meet,
We know it's going to be a treat.
Whatever topic that we see,
We know that we shall all agree.

When we all understand each other,
We're happy having sister, brother.
And know that in the great beyond,
We'll share the joy of friendship's bond.

Bill Robertson 2014

GEORGE

I see him quietly in the hall
Walking slow, but sure and tall.
With outstretched hands we say, "All Hail!"
It's how we greet and never fail.

At times I see him brave the path,
Determined hunter, climbs a strath.
In strong wind and with dampening rain,
Pressing onward, not in vain.

A stalwart ever, through his life,
Successes often, little strife.
A man of courage, straight and fair,
Deserving all of life's good share.

Bill Robertson 2014

Connie and Irv

Connie and Irv we enjoy when we meet
It's especially nice when we sit in their suite.
As the perfect hostess Connie always serves wine,
All feel friendly with the fruit of the vine.

We admire all their effort, they always succeed,
To follow their example is all that we need.
Always together, supporting each other,
Faithful forever as each to their lover.

Bill Robertson 2014

Condo Hunt

Another week and still no news,
It's no surprise I have the "blues".
But soon I hope some dear old lady,
Will sell her house upon a May Day.

A home enjoying a worthy update,
Is just the kind for which we wait.
Ideally on a handsome street,
With properties both fine and neat.

A condo on the topmost floor,
Which sells at four and not much more.
No doubt there's some with ideal space,
But we're too old to run a race.

Although there's lots of time we'll pray,
That soon will come our lucky day.
Our realtor lady's fair and square,
And she has skills beyond compare.

Bill Robertson 2014

Stephen's Green

To live in Sidney by the sea
Is just the place for you and me,
A condo fit for any queen
Can e'er be found at Stephen's Green.

The guy who built nine-nine-five zero
Without a doubt he is a hero.
He built it well in every way,
Ensuring it stands for many a day.

In walking down the length of Fourth
We saw its quality and worth,
Its colour, style did both reveal
A character which did appeal.

The residents we all did meet
When Biddy and Helen provided a treat.
With Joe and Lucille, Pearl and Anita
Colin and Jean, Ian and Diana.

Our Strata Council chief is Joe Dubois
He always knows, he is our Roi.
The voice of wisdom and experience
Filled with wit and common sense.

Tis true we come from different roots
Producing fine and varied shoots.
But what we seek most fervently
Is good old-fashioned privacy.

We're friendly folk who've moved around
For many busy years and found,
That is what we want, a peaceful place
Where life can seek a quieter pace.

It seems we've found the home we need
A condo where the lives we lead
Can pass in quietness all serene
With grateful thanks to Stephen Green.

Bill Robertson 2014

The Judaic Queen

Born on an island with a strawberry curl
Her accent was as true as a PEI girl.
When she moved to the mainland it changed with the years
Since then, don't you know, she speaks like her peers.

As a leader of nurses he met her one day
And found her quite different in a quiet mysterious way.
She spoke with a caution as professionals should
But her thoughts were quite clear and well understood.

They went on joint hospital inspections
Needing reports on their detailed reflections.
Her word-perfect memory then came into play
She'd remembered every word that anyone did say.

But one day in nineteen and seventy-three
She moved south-west for a higher fee.
At the Marcus Lawrence in old Cottonwood
This talented lady did all kinds of good.

As the days rolled on she developed a tan
'Til one day he came and a visit began.
He saw the Grand Canyon and some old Hopi sites
And far in the distance the Francisco heights.

They talked of the past and what future could bring
And after some time he offered a ring.
She took plenty of time to make up her mind
Then later in Ottawa the marriage was signed.

In two years of study a Master's she passed
Raising a Johnson Award to the mast.
If he hadn't realised it before, now he knew
He had married a lady with the brain of a Jew.

When later he found that lineage was true
He knew that his brain was behind in the queue.
In research and executive skills she excelled
It emphasised clearly the genes that she held.

In six years she authored the tale of her life
And helped him publish his life full of strife.
In two thousand and twelve she published a novel
All about a Serpent in a basket of trouble.

Her book is a treasure-trove of murder and mayhems
Of ancient Celtic mystery and other worldly realms.
Now he is sure she is far ahead of him
His role is to satisfy her every single whim.

Bill Robertson 2014

Sally Celebration

Sally has reached her three-score and eleven
To be with her is more than a taste of heaven.
A Queen of Wisdom she ever reigns supreme
A Goddess of Intuition she's the cream.

She's also known by some as Lady Tee
And more than that she is a Doggie Wee.
Of course she always is a Lady Dog
A fully-fledged and published Author Dog.

I know I'm honoured with a very Special Dog
Who feeds me by day and sleeps at night like a log.
I married a wife who knows about orders and law
That's why I call her a Teepee-Teepee Top Paw.

Bill Robertson 2014

Robert Tait

Robert Tait is a pleasure to know,
An expert on wealth and where it should go.
His advice on investment is solid and sure,
If you follow his lead you'll never be poor.

He comes from the Borders of Scotia's realm
Where the handling of problems does not overwhelm.
There's nothing too much if you need some advice,
The trickiest question will be solved in a trice.

"Lord Tait" is the star of the PHN corps,
Long may he serve on the Vancouver shore.

Bill Robertson 2014

Cryptos

Last year my best friend passed away
And sad it was that day
For we had shared so much and more
Of life's enriching lore.

His grandsire came from Russia
Where he had served the Tsar
But latterly it all had changed
And soon he was estranged.

His son escaped across the sea
To where he could be free
And soon became an engineer
Happy and free from fear.

The engineer's son my friend he was
With expertise on laws
We worked together long and hard
Success was our reward.

A Jew who works with a crypto guy
Will always go up high,
The answer to all worldly needs
A blend of ideal creeds.

Bill Robertson 2014

Karmic Principle

Karma is God's law of cause and effects
The rod of God punishes Man's defects.
The Karmic Principle points to true happiness
Those who obey are filled with its goodness.

God's silent presence pervades the Cosmic dream
The Uncreated Silence all our thoughts redeem
When our thoughts are stilled in silent peace
Tis then we find God's endless bliss.

Bill Robertson 2014

The Jewish Diaspora

The Jews are diasporic people
You'll find it in the Holy Bible.
Those who from above came down
Their leader he began a town.

They made the Earthlings do the work
And none there were allowed to shirk.
Some became quite educated
And the best of those were sometimes mated.

Abraham was one such mixture
His family soon became a fixture.
They were in fact the heavenly Hebrews
Because their forebears came from Niburu.

They travelled to find a homeland sure
By mountains, rocks and sand dunes lure.
And finding one in Israel
A host of enemies did repel.

But history shows they were opposed
By diverse rogues that they'd supposed
Would give rewards for all they'd done
But who instead gave only none.

Constantine's Christians were hungry for power
Rome assured them this was their hour.
All dissenters were killed by Rome's murderous crews
And then it was time to turn on the Jews.

The Pharisees were appointed to do Rome's bidding
To deal with anyone they wanted ridding.
Jesus' reforms were not what they wanted
And by the thought of it they were haunted.

Jesus was accused of anti-Roman behaviour
But Pilate didn't want to kill their Saviour.
So he stirred the Pharisees so they'd harass
And they shouted, Crucify him! Not Barabbas!

The Roman Catholic Church asked, "Who killed Jesus?"
It must not be Romans for that wouldn't please us.
So they looked all around for someone to shame
And decided the Jews should take all the blame.

Down through the centuries the Jews knew persecution
Some by dispersal, some by execution.
After several centuries the Moslems joined in
Killing a Jew they said is not a sin.

With Hitler and Stalin with evil all filled
Anti-Semitism has boomed and Jews were all killed.
Humans feel guilty and keep pointing the blame
Why is this so, such an unfair game?

Even today persecution continues
Wherever there are Moslems or Catholics near Jews.
Ayatollahs in Iran preach death to Israel
And everyone else shouts, "Jews go to Hell."

In the end there's this question in everyone's mind
Why only to Jews must we be unkind?
The Gentiles are jealous that the Jews have the brains
So they don't give the Jews any thanks for their pains.

Bill Robertson 2014

Aging Boomers

As Boomers reach their elder years
They enter now a vale of tears,
For even those whose life was pure
Must hope to find a helpful cure.

But those who've led a life of sin
Their old men's ails will now begin.
If oft debauched by drink and lust
Their body now begins to rust.

One could in gory foul detail
Recite the woes this will entail.
Suffice to say that heart and lung
Liver and kidneys come unstrung.

All the others less degraded
Live much longer, join the aged.
Most arthritic, not too wise
Needed much more exercise.

Bill Robertson 2014

Hundred and One

Janie Limond's a hundred and one
Put it there if it weighs a ton.
I knew she'd pass a hundred years.
Come join me now and give three cheers.

Yes, Janie dear you've done it again
You're on your way to another ten.
God bless you every night and day
And walk beside you on your way.

Bill Robertson 2014

In Far Off Scotia

In far off Scotia's famous land
A lady dwells in Creggan Bahn.
Twixt Ayr and Doon her home is found
Both near and far she is renowned.

Her centenarian year is past
And friends she knew she did outlast.
But many more come by to chat
Of local news and things like that.

Thus well informed and up to date
On everything in Church and State
She clearly knows what should be done
To keep the world at large well run.

In truth she knows what would be best
To solve the problems east and west.
If those in power would use her views
It would result in much good news.

The wisdom in a long life learned
Reflects experience well earned.
And Janie Limond has that gift
Which gives her world a special gift.

Bill Robertson 2014

Creggan Bahn

At number two on Seafield Road
Is Creggan Bahn, a royal abode.
It is a court of kings and queens
Though at their age it's mainly queens.

Among the queens I know but one
And she long past my loyalty won.
A Limond lady reigns supreme
A life of quality serene.

Now at this court of Creggan Bahn
The care they give is in the van.
Their nursing ladies are a team
Providing care which is supreme.

My wife and I in prayer give thanks
For loving care which far outranks
What Janie might have found elsewhere.
Creggan Bahn's beyond compare.

The nurses who care for Janie each day
Are Ayrshire heroines in every way.
They each deserve much credit and fame
If I knew I'd record each with her name.

To the staff and owner of royal Creggan Bahn
We offer our praises and thanks to a man.
Wherever we go we'll both raise a toast
To Creggan Bahn Court the home with the most.

Bill Robertson 2014

Scottish College Serampore

Swami Paramahansaji
Is my respected guruji
He attended Scots College Serampore
As a Scot this is something I cannot ignore.

Alexander Duff was a Presbyterian missionary
Who created Scots College in the nineteenth century
With the blessing of the Church of Scotland's Assembly
He taught how to think in English fluently.

We Scots who travel far and wide
Are filled with energy, nothing to hide
We make things happen, creating the news
Tis all because we're crypto-Jews.

Bill Robertson 2014

2015

Goodbye Berwick

We lived at the Berwick for several years
Where we mainly felt good but sometimes had tears.
We met a few couples with whom we related
Whose views about life with ours quite equated.

You had to be ambulant with no special care,
And able to eat the dietary fare.
The average ages were 'tween seventy and eighty,
With no major illness or obvious frailty.

The Owner of the home had built it too big,
So he hired an accountant who was told to rejig.
This fellow decided to change all the rules,
Which made us feel we'd been treated like fools.

Admissions on wheelchairs and Walkers galore,
Crowded the elevators, blocking the doors.
Wee dogs and cats were allowed in as pets
Complaints went unheeded, you might get regrets.

Dozens of Walkers crowded the aisles,
No time for chatting, no time for smiles.
He lowered some rentals, packed every suite,
Ours remained high so he appeared like a cheat.

We decided to move to our own little place,
To lower the costs and quieten the pace.
It took us a year and quite a long look,
'Til we found our own condo, our own little nook.

Bill Robertson 2015

Spring 2015

We finally retired to 302 on Fourth Street,
Our little home in Sidney-by-the Sea.
The owner took our offer at the outset which
At that time was the best that we could get.
And once we were in we found the size was right.
Moving is a challenge, of that there is no doubt
And we'll have lots to test us before the year is out.
A rising PSA with a growing HGPIN
Could be a word of comfort or a punch upon the chin.

Bill Robertson 2015

To Janie

Oh I remember days long past
When we four shared a royal repast.
With Tom and Fay and you and me
We all enjoyed a "Hillside Tea".

Tom Limond, Ayrshire's 'King' elect
His tall figure commanded respect.
A man you could trust, his word was his bond.
Problems were solved when he waved his hand.

Fay Limond worked hard every day
She was mostly quiet but did have her say.
Janie and Fay both helped with the "Tea",
Which was mainly consumed by Tom and by me.

We solved all the problems of Church and of State
And others as well which are hard to relate.
We laughed and we chuckled, we had a good chat,
I ate so much I was going to get fat.

In some ways it feels it was just yesterday
I recall what was said like it was just today.
Yes Janie and Tom and Fay and me,
We were all just as happy as a family can be.

Bill Robertson 2015

Dearest Janie

Janie Limond is a hundred and two
It seems like a dream but it's really quite true.
She has lived for most of a century past
And most of her peers she still does outlast.

Now she has entered the 21st Age
And is well on the way into that stage.
Her wisdom and knowledge have much they could say
To guide younger people along their life's way.

We live in a time of challenge and change
With some who our values seek to derange.
But basics are standards which we should not throw out
And Janie's are those that we should shout out.

So Janie moves into another great year
It's a time that we send her a warm loving cheer.
By her strength she prevails and we love her forever
Our friendship remains which time will not sever.

Bill Robertson 2015

Wearisome Woman or Shady Lady

She arrived in town with thoughts that were sinister
Applying to a church who were in need of a minister.
She judged that the Session were worthy old souls
Who would trust her ability to meet all their goals.

Once appointed she seemed like an honest believer
But in time she behaved more a rogue, a deceiver.
It began with her stretching the rules on vacation
As she disappeared for times of lengthening duration.

The history of churches show good times and bad
In today's morality some churches get had.
The details of stipends need review and revision
In times of decay and evil ambition.

This woman has shown no respect for authority
Nor displayed a scintilla of moral integrity.
That she sits in the choir is a piece of impertinence
Whoever allowed it should show shame and some penitence.

God helps the helpless has been said in the past.
With recent good news one hopes it will last.
"Faith without works" is the best of advice
Forget not the works or it can be not nice.

Bill Robertson 2015

To Sally

Oh love that shares your life with me
With selfless service fills each day.
Without you now where would I be
I surely would have lost my way.

Before we met my life was bleak
So many things were turning sour.
My strengths were down and seeming weak
Until your love renewed my power.

And then as months passed into years
Our lives rebounded day by day.
We conquered trials and calmed our fears
We formed a team and found a way.

And now as we reach years mature
Our souls unite in daily prayer
We're happy neither rich nor poor
We've learned the truth of saying, 'Take care'.

Bill Robertson 2015

Coryza 2015

On the sixth day of a nasty 'flu I hadn't had one in five years,
No doubt the anti-Vaccination crowd were enjoying a chorus of leers
I'm feeling a little bit better today but still not out of it yet.
She has ordered me to stay in bed and I feel like an old pampered pet.
An old nurse they say is always right but I don't like being ordered about
So I'm feeling quite growly and definitely owly and almost ready to pout.
But wisdom steps in and keeps me from sin, 'cos I don't want to hurt my beloved
So there's nothing to do but sit tight and sit quiet awaiting the freedom I covet.
I'm dogged if nothing else she said and prayer that too would be good
I agreed with that thought to do what I ought and decided to do what I should.

Bill Robertson 2015

Flu 2015

Breakfast in bed as usual is small but that's just as it should be
Through the rest of the day she plied me with food which I ate
    from lunchtime to tea.
My loud bouts of coughing and unpleasant spluttering I continue
    for most of the day
But still she says little, for we both know the score so what is
    there more we could say?
My frequent attacks of sneezing and wheezing I prefer to try and
    prevent
With both careers in Sickness we exchange looks and agree to
    make no further comment.
As a dedicated nurse she treats me so well, 'til I see she has the
    bug too
And we both realise and it's not a surprise there are no perfect
    vaccines for 'flu'.
As always we wondered about what we had missed to prevent
Who did we meet to talk or change hands, or maybe it just really
    was meant.

Bill Robertson 2015

Reincarnation

My happy soul abides forever
Death's ending trials it faces never.
For all mankind is everlasting
Which does not arise by prayer or fasting.

Man's life on Earth is like a flower
It blooms awhile then loses power.
The mind and body surely dies
But spirit onward ever flies.

All that was and is shall ever be
Our spirits live in one futurity.
Although our minds and bodies die
Each Earthly life, it flies on bye.

Our spirits live in perpetuity
While up in heaven they're sipping tea.
Until it is time to wend our way
To another Reincarnation day.

Bill Robertson 2015

Reincarnation Ideas

Never in all futurity shall any one of us not exist.
We have bloomed once before in the garden of life.
We abide in formless form in Spirit's everlastingness.
To reincarnation thither do we wend again.
Man's soul, the true soul, is everlasting.
All that is and has been shall ever be.
All of mankind has existed forever and will continue to exist to all futurity.
We have all bloomed before in the garden of life and thither do we wend again.
God's everlasting spirit in which we abide in formless form forever.
Our souls do ever abide in Spirit's everlastingness.
Perpetuity/Endless time/Perpetual/abiding.

Bill Robertson 2015

The Special Year

This year has seen a timely change
Some expected, some quite strange.
Reaching on to eighty-five
I'm happy to be still alive.

Trying to keep my body fit
Was not so easy, I admit.
At Seniors Games I threw with grit
It now seems I may have to quit.

But I'll enjoy throwing Hammer and Weight
It makes me feel it's not too late
To reach the standard for my age
And turn for me another page.

I also like the Discus and Weight
Though not so good, they both do rate.
So thus I try to keep afloat
And keep on sailing in my boat.

The details of my genetic frame
Provided info on my name.
Which proved a fact I never knew
That I am certainly a Jew.

At first this was a big surprise
But soon I understood the ties
Which linked me to Ashkenazi Jews
Which is for me such happy news.

From 2010 to 2013 I studied long and hard
The Swami's heavenly teaching was all of my reward
Paramahansi Yogananda is my guruji
And I became a Kriya Yogi, October 2013.

And since that time my meditation
Has brought me into Self-Realization.
My soul has found a wondrous release
A bliss which brings perpetual peace.

Kriya Yogi Bill Robertson 2015

Father's Day

Starfish and sea shells with love on Father's Day
Nothing could be better is all I have to say.

A time of celebration, our family's own sensation
A blessing from above, with those I'll always love.

Bill Robertson 2015

Prostatic Probing

Doctor Stenhoff likes biopsies
To review my cancer "popsies".
He says if over eighty years
We're all prostatic cancer peers.

I like the thought of fellowship
It makes me feel I'm really hip.
Until that last, that final day
We'll stand together, share the way.

Although he said in tone quite brightly
My death by cancer was unlikely.
He needs to keep a friendly eye
On what will be the way I die.

And so from time to time 'behind'
He probes to see what he can find.
Necrotic tissue may be there
Within the gland's old capsule layer.

That specimen's help he will enlist
And send to a pathologist.
One hopes the findings which present
Are innocent and wholly pleasant.

But if the test shows cancer spread
And that I'll likely soon be dead.
At least it will provide synopsis
And stop the need for more biopsies.

Bill Robertson (Retired doctor) 2015

Coronary Memory

I never thought it would happen to me
As always I felt as fit as a flea.
I got caught with a weight which was too much to lift
And ended up with a coronary 'rift'.

If it hadn't been for my wonderful wife
Her skill and quick action was what saved my life.
She got me the care and the treatment I needed
And the doctor whose consummate skill then succeeded.

I had travelled from home to the Sampan and back
Then on to the Jubilee like a cat in a sack.
Then Doctor Siega with consummate ease
Inserted two stents with hardly a squeeze.

To where I go now it's quite hard to tell
I hope to survive and not go to hell.
It's a challenge for sure which I must just accept
And fight to improve and not be inept.

But before I get cocky on upping my life
I now have a date with a surgeon's knife.
He says it should work and I fully agree
As anything else I would not like to see.

But this forecast was mixed if truth it be told
As a fate such as that I'd hate to behold.
For it sounded quite nasty as he did portend
And rather unpleasant and no way to end.

But I keep optimistic with regard to my life
And I hope to live long with my dear little wife.
We are best friends forever, it's a wonder we share
For we've learned over years the best way to care.

Bill Robertson 2015

Post-coronary

From September to December
Is the busiest time of the year
I'll be having lots of treatment
Just in time for Christmas cheer.

First I'll see my friendly GP
So he knows just where I'll be
Then I'll need to see a 'veep'
Who will make me go to sleep.

But before I face the knife
There's the guy who saved my life
A cardiologist most skilled
Who'll decide if I get 'drilled'

Then at last it's time to see
My urologist, yes he
Dr. Steinhoff with his scope
Will transfix me in the hope

That my 'channels' will be clear
And be used without a fear
That I end up with a 'block'
And become a useless crock.

I have hopes I will be better
And become a record setter.

Bill Robertson 2015

Relationships at Work

Sometimes in life we feel supreme
And come to believe our thoughts are cream.
Being highly trained and qualified
We must not ever be deprived.

When egos get a bit inflated
And others views are underrated.
That's the time to stop and think
Before we bring things to the brink.

When working with colleagues as part of a team
It's best to be calm and never to scream.
Each member deserves some time to reflect
And all are worthy of equal respect.

Now whether you're high or low in rank
Or know you have more or less in the bank.
Be kind to the folk that you meet each day
And your lives will get better in every way.

Bill Robertson 2015

Trust

As I look around the world today
The power of trust seems gone away.
So often in the daily news
All we hear is journalist's views.

In Canada in two thousand one hundred and fifteen
It seems they've gotten afraid of being seen.
Our freedoms increased with Trudeau's Charter
But lawyers can argue and give them no quarter.

The media now say their reports are "alleged"
For fear that a lawyer gets them legally wedged.
Or they talk of "suspicions" that might have been said
And sometimes it's "suggestions" that are used instead.

While the Charter gives the right to confidentiality
They're now more interested in avoiding reality.
Trudeau gave them freedom to spend 'til they dropped.
If they still believe a liar they'll again get bopped.

Too many still believe in the religion of conformity
And keep following the mass, the sheep-like majority.
They had better get a shepherd who can keep them all on track
Or they'll end up in chaos at the mercy of the pack.

When will the Boomers and generations "X" and "Y"
Reinstate truth before they all die?
They need to face facts and the truths of reality
If they hope to succeed in today's society.

Bill Robertson 2015

Talking

When a man is young or old
And feels an urgent need to speak out bold,
Tis wiser oft to have a thought,
And not go talking lots of rot.

I know from personal experience
To use a little common sense.
Sometimes a word that's out of turn
Can surely cause ones ears to burn.

If one intends a telling fact
Be sure it is said with careful tact.
There is no point being harsh and hurtful
But always say what's fair and truthful.

While words of wisdom express good
And guide us towards a worthwhile mood.
Though they inspire us on our way
It's what we do that wins the day.

Bill Robertson 2015

2016

Old Not Bold

Oh Janie I am growing old
It's not a time to be too bold.
If I should die at eighty-seven
I'll find a place up there in heaven.

I'm sure there'll be a seat for me
Where I can sit and have some tea.
I'll book two seats for you and Sally
And a comfy blanket for our dog Toby.

We'll sit and chat for hours on end
On how the world is going to end.
We'll solve all problems one by one
It surely will be lots of fun.

Singing in the Heavenly Choir
You and Sally will never tire.
But I have karma to resolve
To Earthly life I must revolve.

In time I'll get to stay in heaven
And join you two in easy livin'.
Until that time dear Toby waits
To greet me at the heavenly gates.

Bill Robertson 2016

The Divine Attributes

Attributes of God which bless
The first of these is Fearlessness.
Next to that she does impart
The wondrous gift, Purity of heart.

She preaches wisdom and no less
Guides her realm with Steadfastness.
When bells of need begin to ring
She answers all with Almsgiving.

When weaklings fall to sins' dark taint
She shows the power of Self-restraint.
With devout oblations in her sights
She follows all Religious Rites.

Her righteous leadership endures
In study of God's true Scriptures.
And where are things so full of sin
We need to up our Self-discipline.

Sincerity we all confess
She demonstrates Straightforwardness.
We must avoid harming with fury
While she leads the world in Non-injury.

Anger results from the evil path
She leads the way by absence of Wrath.
What does she say on this forsooth
The worlds we know are built on Truth.

The majority lust to win by a ton
Her path is one of Renunciation.
And knowing a sense of new release
She is united to the God of Peace.

No Calumny or evil slander
Will upset or circumvent her
With Compassion towards all beings
She displays her noble feelings.

Having mastered evil Greed
She supports all those in need.
With pure and kindly Gentleness
She seeks to help those in distress.

Showing always Modesty
She shares her powerful energy.
Helping those with Restlessness
Find tranquil peace and heaven's bless.

Awareness of God's cosmic fire
And Radiance of character
She reaches out preventing pain
Forgiveness queen knows only gain.

With Patience bear misfortune rude
And face life's ills with fortitude.
In Cleanliness of body and mind
She respects God's spirit kind.

Non-hatred brings the ideal day
With lack of Conceit, the perfect way.
Now she supports non-hating ways
To blow away conceit's bad days.
…and who is She?

Bill Robertson 2016

The Return

The Return will come what'ere the date
We Earthlings do not clearly know our fate
God is watching while we wait
He knows if it be soon or late.

Extra-terrestrials from Niburu planet
Came to Earth by plane and jet
For gold they knew they had to get
And made us slaves with scant regret.

Long brutal years we Earthlings toiled
Our lives were harsh our bodies soiled.
But Niburites pursued their search
Nought could stop their gold research.

If they had foresworn their plan
We'd not have had our Earthly span.
Our history would then be nought
And all we did not worth a jot.

That's not at all the way it went
We progressed far with strong intent.
With Anu's help from time to time
We all achieved progress sublime.

610 BC was when they left
At first we felt we were bereft.
But we did not succumb to depression
In fact we made a vast progression.

And now the next Return is nigh
The pundits say they do not lie.
Anu's planet is dark, dark red
It's coming from the south tis said.

Keep an eye towards south-west
That direction will be best.
When it comes within our range
Then you'll know there will be change.

Bill Robertson 2016

Cheating

Cheating has long been a human sin
Since Jacob stole a blessing from his kin.

As professionals here and there compete
Some often take a chance and cheat.
Once they gain their client's trust
Too soon they follow money's lust.

When they work for government fees
They oft can do what ere they please.
One knows of doctors, what a bunch
Sharing cheating fees, at lunch.

Now since Soviet days of yore
Cheating in sport has reached the core.
In FIFA and the IOC
Corruption is there for all to see.

Whenever there's political gain
Coaches and refs. oft do their best
Illegal penalties to obtain
To satisfy their greedy quest.

Just recently at Rio Games
German football's acting dames
Were quick to take well-acted falls
And thereby gain illegal goals.

Honest athletes will opt out
And fill the public's mind with doubt.
I hope that youth will then rebel
And send the cheaters all to Hell.

Bill Robertson 2016

Poem to Toutou

She is my dear little doggie
My beloved, above all, the best.
At night at prayer I hold her hand
And together we share peace of the soul.

Every day we meditate together
And find our soul's peace and bliss
Which gives us endless joy.
We live in life-long peace.

Bill Robertson 2016

Poeme de Toutou

Elle est mon cher petit toutou
Ma bien-aimee surtout le mieux.
En nuit en prieres je lui donne la main
Et partage ensemble tranquillite de l'ame.

Tous les jours nous faisons nos meditations
Et trouvent cette paix et beatitude de l'ame
Ce que nous donne la joie sans bornes
Et vivent en paix n'importe comment.

Bill Robertson 2016

2017

People in India

As we go out about our day
We meet some people on our way.
Some may smile in our direction
While other's eyes make no connection.

I met a man whose eye was bright
His smile was friendly, warm as light.
He was a leper from Tibet
The happiest one I'd seen as yet.

Another time, another place
An outstretched hand, a practiced face,
Demanding Backsheesh for a licence.
Stoic-faced, I left in silence.

In Ranipet on my first day
Balasunderam's welcome way
Sealed a friendship short, not long
He to Dubai, I to Kalimpong.

Up in the hills I met Ongmeet
A nurse and matron, skilled complete.
Married soon to Sikkim gone
The surgeon there, her only son.

And I remember Rakham Singh
We met in India in the spring.
He had a steady eye with no fears
We worked together, four busy years.

He later went to live in Sikkim
From Cobble Hill I corresponded with him.
Over fifty years later we shared things that mattered
Most whole and worthy, some quite tattered.

Pastor Noptering Malamoo I met
On a day I will surely not forget.
Up in the hills near Bhutan
Stayed at his home, a complete man.

Next day we met some Khamba escapees
Just out of Tibet where they'd fought the Chinese.
Noptering raised a chopi like the sword of the Spirit
Hoping Tibet's freedom would come by the power of it.

Long hours of surgery at the hospital's OR
Gracie Mary Rai ran it all like a star.
To thank her again for all that she did
I send that to heaven where her spirit is hid.

Dr. Albert Craig I met on a stair
His look was blank-faced, an ugly stare.
All he wanted was for me to go
Obviously he saw me as a deadly foe.

Dr. Karmakar was a friend
Who betimes some help did lend.
He gave an ether anaesthetic
To a patient at the clinic.

Jaitee and Pratap were ever faithful.
No trials at home did them deter.
Both Nepali Hindus they
We all went happily on our way.

Rev. Ellis Shaw stuck in my craw.
His lies and cheats against the law.
The job he called me to was not
And what was left was only rot.

Dr. Janet Duncan tried her best
To keep Craig happy in his nest.
But sad to say it didn't work,
He left her cold, oh what a jerk.

Our kindly Munshi Jeevanasen
Ensured our Tamil graduation.
Read it, write it, pray it, do it,
Jeevas taught us how to say it.

The Rani Dorje was supreme
In Kalimpong she was the Queen.
She sent her staff to me for care
And all she did was good and fair.

B.C. Simick from Nepal
Taught his language to us all.
He tutored me some evenings long
And soon I spoke like Kalimpong.

Lisbet ran the surgical wards
She helped by teaching me Nepali words.
So I could talk with the words she had given.
She's now seventy-seven or maybe in heaven.

The sisters Simick were nurses terrific
Their standards of work were truly prolific.
No matter the day, the month or the hour
They were ready to help to the extent of their power.

Bill Robertson 2017

Soli's Sweet Soul

Since ere I met you years ago
Your spirit's strength I'll always know
Betokens kindly warm true fellowship
The sign and seal of spirit's friendship.

And where can such a bond be found?
Tis rare to meet within Earth's bound.
But once we know it's soul refreshing
We thank our God for such a blessing.

Where in this life can peace be found
And kindness flow on all around?
Soli's sweet soul will always be
A gift to all, a joy to me.

Bill Robertson 2017

Bill Robertson

Sounds of Sidney

In Sidney one hears condo sounds
Well before the morning rounds.
When citizens all want to sleep
Enjoying the peace of slumber deep.

But suddenly a seagull's shriek
Emits from out its gaping beak.
Destroying whatever peace was had
By noisy squawks both bad and sad.

In springtime seagull broods keep moaning
Which leaves one quite upset and groaning.
Far too many seagulls are here
Time they are culled like a herd of deer.

At 6:20 am there's the Purolator plane
It roars with a sound like an old express train.
Which is good and reminds one it's time to arise
And get on with some work and trying to be wise.

On a different track there's the problem of hoot
Which doves make each morn with their special toot-toot.
It's nice that these doves all chat with their mates
Every morning and evening they keep their toot dates.

By noon the sparrows invade with their twitters
Which one has to admit always gives one the jitters.
There are quite a few crows swooping down with loud caws
Who don't seem to know there are anti-noise laws.

Maybe the noisiest things are the grass-cutters
They should all be silenced and stop all my mutters.
And through the day busses go by all a rumbling
On their way to the ferry with groaning and grumbling.

Hourly jet planes pass over their engines a roaring
To far off destinations they speed off a soaring.
Then garbage trucks come with much crashing and banging
Unloading their stuff with much beeping and clanging.

Then comes the sound of mindless selfishness
When a woman forgets which switch to press
Leaving her horn to continuous blaring
But she walks to her condo without even caring.

Thoughtless young men dumping their garbage
Throwing in their loads like kids in a rage.
Late night police cars sirens a wailing
Chasing a speeder that they are a tailing.

Now and again a lone dog keeps barking
Wanting back in after some larking.
Or a tomcat fight with two toms snarling
Setting old scores in a midnight quarrelling.

Less disturbing are times when the neighbours are chatting
In conversation pleasant without any ratting.
And sometimes of a night some passersbys come clinging
Each to each other as they wander home singing.

Bill Robertson 2017

Holding the Mail in Sidney

Christmas comes but once a year
Full of mail and Christmas cheer.
Packages we love the most
All on time by Canada Post.

Such wondrous service is the boast
Of every mailman on the coast.
However all of them admit
Sometimes a snag can cause a fit.

As an oldie myself I do admit
We can cause problems which test the wit.
Of lady and gentlemen Posties all
Who'd rather have none of these problems at all.

It is all to do with Holding the Mail
Which oldies like me hope will prevail.
So that all the parcels that we've been sent
Arrive at our home just as they were meant.

But that's where the problems begin to arise
Cos oldies like me fail to realize
That we're getting so old that our memory's goin'
And we're sometimes not sure if we're suckin' or blowin'

We appear at the Office saying "I know they've been sent
If I don't get them now I won't be content."
Or maybe a neighbour was going to do it,
But sadly forgot and instead he just blew it.

And sometimes the neighbour he trusted forgot,
And seeing all the goodies had taken the lot.
While others on seeing them were quite filled with doubt
And thinking it junk threw it all out.

Our Posties are noble we love all they do
I'll try to remember to be good too.
If you think we can help just give us a shout
And if we remember we'll help without doubt.

An old Oldie, not a Boomer, Not a Generation X,
Not a Generation Y and not a Millennial 2017

God-given Blessing

Hardworking and dedicated, unselfish to a fault
A lady ever-caring and on this Earth, the salt.
As wife and mother ever appreciated
She is blessed as God-created.

Ever loving, ere forgiving
Her wisdom is needed, ever living.
Of Doctorate intelligence
And overflowing common sense

A lady of sublime intuition
Who ere foresees the right decision.
Of outlook always quietly hopeful
With strong ambition still the rule.

A God-believing determined soul
Kindly, wise her happy goal.
Always praiseworthy and deserving
Full of joy and ere unswerving.

Bill Robertson 2017

A Rest for Sally

Sally always does her best
My darling wife she's ever blest.
At times I wonder how she's doing
And if there is a problem brewing.

It could be something unexpected
Needing still to be detected.
Maybe she needs to see a doctor
To find out what may have assailed her.

She has been working very hard
Upon a project all regard
As worthwhile at the highest level
And worthy of a time of revel.

But I accept it could be serious
Something more or less injurious.
In my own view she's always blest
And all she needs is lots of rest.

Bill Robertson 2017

Tara's Gate

Oh Tara's Gate on Erin's isle
It lies in Meath's most tranquil mile.
And those to whom the key is known
The way to Tir-na-n-og is shown.

And many seek that blessed land
Where peace and love walk hand in hand.
Its people walk in wisdom's way
That's where I long to go and stay.

Bill Robertson 2017

Associate Dean – Greg

A leader is one who has wisdom and courage
With great strength of mind and first class knowledge.
Hard working and dependable in crisis situations
Cool clear in mind and a steel-strong patience.

Approachable and sympathetic in all kinds of discussion
Wise in flexibility and appropriate compassion.
Humble in victory, calm in defeat
A man for all seasons, a leader complete.

Old Bill (Dad) 2017

Lord Robert

Expert advice on all kinds of investing
"Lord Robert" achieves it without ever resting.
Such dedicated service he provides with a smile
It's all part of his friendly professional style.

Utter dependability gives customer bliss
Hard-working service with nothing amiss.
Long-term proven sympathy towards client needs
With speedy responses he ere intercedes.

My trusty advisor from P.H.N.
He still is now and was so then.
Over sixty years of investing alone
He is the best I have ever known.

Sir William Robertson 2017

Getting Old

I'm getting old, it won't be long before I'm gone
Before I sing my final song.
I've done my best in East and West
And hope to pass in Heaven's test.

When we end our Earthly way
Our minds and bodies pass away.
But spirits stay in life eternal
Escaping from the place infernal.

It won't be long before I'm gone
I'd rather wait till after dawn.
The best of times for me to go
Is in the early evening's glow.

But if it better suits your way
I'll try and die at break of day.
So you can call the burial place
Where I have booked a comfy space.

Have no concern I'll be upset
For there in Heaven I will be met
By Toby's friendly paw and lick.
In fact it will be just the trick.

But let's be clear this is no joke
I'm talking about our "after croak".
God made Heaven a place for review
Where He decides what we need to renew.

He sends us to a new location
Where we can have an education.
On how to live a moral life
Instead of depending on our wife.

It's all about Reincarnation
Where God sends us to a probation.
In truth it is our blessed chance
To help our spirit to advance.

If we can thus improve our karma
And make our life show better dharma
Then we'll be happy and rejoice
That we have made a better choice.

We'll have to travel many times
To distant planets, different climes.
But in the end it will be best
And help us reach our Heavenly quest.

One day I hope to reach that shore
Where I can endless God adore.
I know I'll have some time to wait
It would be nice to know the date.

Bill Robertson 2017

Behaviour in 21st Century Canada

Behaviour in Canada is going down the tubes
It started with the Boomers who committed many boobs.
They decided it was time to throw away the rules
And let kids behave like a bunch of spoiled brat fools.

So generation X believed it was their right
To give up on good manners and become a nasty blight.
With greed, lust and selfishness as their cardinal objectives
And the help of the Press letting them cruise on invectives.

Such a turn of events is so vile and intense
It establishes a pattern of lasting offence.
The generations X and Y and all millennials too
Must take responsibility and decide what they must do.

It's true not all Canadians have thrown their morals out
So surely it is time to ensure it's not in doubt,
By people with good standards declaring their moral views
And rescuing all of Canada from bad behaviour blues.

Bill Robertson 2017

Today's Callow Ways

Afar I see life's callow way
Where selfish egos hold their sway.
Funding rowdies in their pay
To deny what experts say.

Environmental air-heads, radicals
As life-long teenager left-wing liberals
Scientific half-truth nonsense
Spouting forth as proven truth.

What can be done to renew the truth?
Return to us a moral balance,
Where wisdom reigns instead of fantasy
And mankind regains a sense of tolerance.

Bill Robertson 2017

Good Character Qualities

Character is something we all admire
A quality to which we all aspire.
Its fundamental power relies
On one's ability to be wise.

The key to happiness is dependable caring
Combined with love and blissful sharing.
It's good when people are calm and forgiving
And helps to keep smooth our way of living.

It's helpful that we do things both helpful and kindly
And better if we do them routinely and blindly.
Whatever is done should always be lively
With actions useful and valued quite highly.

A person who knows is both valued and knowledgeable
And possesses the facts which are clear and believable.
We like an approach that seems worthy and credible
Especially one which is clearly achievable.

I really like a guy who is competent
Hardworking, faithful, resolute and provident.
The coming world needs those who are intuitive
Filled with understanding both practical and sensitive.

We shall need lots of people who are tough and courageous
Filled with ideas and sometimes pugnacious.
One who has foresight, tact and determination
A reasonable manager filled with imagination.

To complete this review we'll need downright honesty
And thoughts which are filled with shining creativity.

Bill Robertson 2017

Headin' North

One day in October I dreamed of going forth
Where a wolf can find home in the snow of the north.
So we're going away to the land of the Bear
Where soon we'll be finding a suitable lair.

The Wolf and the Bear have much they can share
On the best place to live and the clothes one should wear.
As it's twenty-five years since I lived in the cold,
And it could be quite chilly, or so I've been told.

We've been lookin' at info Katrina has given
On houses in places where we might be livin'.
I know she'll be lookin' out dens for the Bear
While lookin' around for an ideal Wolf's lair.

So when 2018 comes along, we plan to be there
Aheadin' up north to be close to the Bear.
We'll be chattin' and snackin' with nothin' to spare
It's just what we do, the Wolf and the Bear.

Bill Robertson 2017

Moving

Some months ago I had a thought
Of things to do and when and what.
Our lives have still a bit to go
Before we meet the final foe.

Was where we live the place to be?
Or had we somewhere else to see?
I'm near the end but Sally's not.
Where should she be and why and what?

I knew the answer in a trice
Twas near our son that would be nice.
He is now Associate Dean
Organizing the Research scene.

In Edmonton city is where he's based
And that's where now we should be placed.
So that's the objective which we've made
It's time to be no more delayed.

Our son has helped us find Katrina
A virtual Realtor ballerina.
She has given a selection
Which meets our needs to a perfection.

We're going to meet her in over a week
When of some homes we'll have a good peek.
Katrina's fine skills will give us a lead
Next year, to find the one that we need.

Bill Robertson 2017

2018

Sidney Seagull

He soars above the bustling streets
Squawking at every bird he meets.
Betimes he finds a place to rest
On which he plans to make a nest.

A ruling monarch of the sky
Demands a site both safe and high.
Now Sidney is a thriving place
Where condos fill each vacant space.

There soon with ease he ends his quest
A condo roof he finds is best.
And there a roost both flat and wide
He chooses for his chirping bride.

Tis springtime and the time is ripe
So soon a host of chicklings pipe
But condo owners through the night
Find the sound a sleepless blight.

As noisy seagulls fill the air
What can be done and what is fair?
There's some like me who've begun to mull
The time has come to have a cull!

Bill Robertson 2018

A Final Home

We've been in this condo a hundred days
Finding out the local ways.
The people here are busy working
This is no place for any shirking.

It's summer time, the days are warm
The trees are clothed in leafy charm.
Atop the ridge of a deep ravine
A lazy trail defines the scene.

When winter comes there will be snow
Just how deep we don't yet know.
No doubt we'll get a goodly share
But snugly found, we just won't care.

Bill Robertson 2018

Settling In

I've arrived and survived and I'm still quite alive
Like a bee getting used to a different beehive.
Edmonton city's a big kinda town
And we're feeling the need for some time to calm down.

We've moved many times in both of our lives
And this is the biggest we're trying to survive.
As I'm now in my nineties it becomes pretty clear
That we'll still be unpacking by the end of the year.

But this gives us both time to research other things
And decide when and where we should stretch out our wings.
Sally I'm sure will continue to write
I shall write poems, some heavy some light.

The weather here they say can be quite hot or cold
And it's sunnier than BC is what we've been told.
In West Creek I'm enjoying some time in the sun
Twenty minutes is good if it's not overdone.

Some days we go shopping as we still have to eat
The variety of stores is really a treat.
As our West Creek house is quite a bit bigger
A little bit more is what we must figure.

With advice on whatever we still might need
We'll be ready and know just how to proceed.
Searching for stools or a table or seat
'Til we find what seems right and really complete.

Bill Robertson 2018

Greg as Always

I've lived here and there in the East and the West
Met all kinds of men throughout my life's quest.
Most were quite good, though a few turned out bad
But the best of them all is the one calls me Dad.

Since we first walked together it's now many years
And we talk about life as it affects our careers.
Though we've lived different lives we always agree
I with him, he with me.

We live now together in the same old town
And we often meet at home or downtown.
Taking one day at a time is our thought for the day
And we'll keep close together whatever the way.

Bill Robertson 2018

Birthday Blast

He's at his fifty year Birthday blast
At UNB he rarely was outclassed.

In all his jobs he never was surpassed
About his work if ever he is asked
He humbly says that it was truly vast.

In future with his colours on the mast
He'll venture always on from first to last.

If life goes on a bit too fast
He may just sit upon his ass!

Old Bill (Dad) 2018

As Sally Is

Oh how she is loved, my Sally dear,
In so many ways she does endear.
A lady kind and very special
Always true, always helpful.

Where there's a need she's quickly there
A loving spirit offering care.
Whatever the hour whatever the day
She's there to help in any way.

I love this lady deep and truly
It's what I feel and that quite fully.
For as long as I live that's the way it will be
These are my thoughts, the message from me.

Bill Robertson 2018

Mumbling and Grumbling is Really Quite Humbling

As passing years increase my age
Soon comes the time to turn the page.
A man is wise appearing humble
Than seeing all his dreams to crumble.

From day to day I do my best
To banish trouble from our nest.
Avoiding any stupid fumble
Which could our dreams and plans to tumble.

My hearing now is on the wane
And may need help which could explain
What now is sounding like a bumble
And puts all hearing in a jumble.

And now as memory begins to fade
Confusing thoughts my mind invade.
When all I hear is just a mumble
There's nothing left to do but grumble.

Bill Robertson 2018

Hearing Aids

I'm old and grey and getting white
And mainly sleep five hours a night.
My eyes are good, my brain is clear
But there are sounds I cannot hear.

I went to get a hearing test
From Dr. Quarti, he is best.
He prescribed a Hearing Aid
And now I'm trying it, as he said.

After ten days the volume went down
I replaced the battery, which gave me more sound.
And the ProWax minifit filter and dome.
So then I heard clearly and knew I was home.

When my trial test is over I've thought it all over
I will purchase the miniRITE and thus be in clover.
After that maybe plan for a party
In honour for one, a Dr. Marc Quarti.

Bill Robertson 2018

Belief

I'm eighty-eight and now feel free
To talk of my belief.
It's time for me to tell my tale
God grant that it be brief.

Presbyterian born was I
My parents went to church.
In Sunday school and in the choir
I made my contribution.

As time went by I pleased the Session
They then made me an Elder.
My religion interest much enhanced
I felt I should advance it.

I just missed being in World War II
But had to serve the Military.
For two good years I served the Force
Declining a fine commission.

My long-term plan was Medicine
With lengthy years of study.
By God's good grace I made the grade
And thus became a doctor.

I'd missed the War but felt the need
To help the sick and suffering
And volunteered for Mission work
Wherever it was needed.

The Mission sent me out to India
A land with many sick
And healing those in Jesus' name
Fulfilled a noble goal.

For seven long years of goodly challenge
I served the people there.
Til God called locals to the work
And so replacing me.

In 1963 Revision!
My life plan changed severely
From Orthopedics to General Practice
And on to Health Admin.

My leaving the world of Clinical Practice
Seemed such a tragedy
But with no funds from missionary years
I had to act with dispatch.

I still believed in Almighty God
And still volunteered as an Elder.
But that all religions should be one
Was what should now be done.

My search to survive with a family of five
Took me over to Canada's shore.
But the mother of three had enough of me
And she left me with daughters three.

Busy years passed with experience vast
And my life was changing again
For I found a good wife, the joy of my life
And I knew I was blessed from that day.

At over eighty years old I still searched on
For direct communion with God
And was blessed to find a Swami who knew
And taught me just what I should do.

Paramahansa Yogananda is my guru
In Scientific Meditation he showed me how
With Sally my wife we meditate each day
And we know we are closer to God.

All mankind should meditate to God every day
That's the message we give on our way.
As yogis we know it's the way all should know
And we'll follow that path till we go.

Bill Robertson 2018

Religious Development

I believe in God from first to last
And stick my colours to that mast.
But different faiths have flagged my way
Leading to my faith today.

A Presbyterian from the start
Much Scripture I could quote by heart.
In time I was an Elder made
For fifty years I toiled unpaid.

Ten years in India as a Medical Mish,
I saw multiple faiths, as many as you'd wish.
Learned about Hindus, Sikhs and Parsees
Moslems, Buddhists, Jains and Jews.

Basically I found them all the same
Belief in God with a different name.
Most date back for two thousand years
Helping people overcome their fears.

Much further back in Yuga cycle
Hindu rishis found something vital.
Direct communion with the Spirit of God
Meditation by Kriya Yoga achieved it.

Bill Robertson 2018

Today's Standards

Approaching heaven's golden gate
I think of what I should relate
To those I'll have to leave behind.
What thoughts to them I should remind.

As I look out at life today
There's lots of things I'd like to say.
But time is short, I must be brief
And concentrate on which are chief.

The Western world is full of change
With problems great and small and strange.
I'll mention only just a few
On which I have a special view.

With Canada's moral standards falling
The overall picture is appalling.
The Boomers began it in the sixties and seventies
No one could stop it, not even the Mounties.

Generations X and Y and Millennials too
All spoiled rotten except for a few.
They've created an age of total entitlement
Fulfilling their demands for perpetual contentment.

Already we're seeing how the wind is blowing
Canada's moral tone is gradually falling.
Lying and cheating is now largely the rule
And freed sexual relations are regarded as 'cool'.

Municipal school education has slid into a slump
And young student literacy has dropped with a bump.
School curriculums have now got to be fun
And the kids don't learn how anything's done.

The latest sign of moral decrepitude
Is marijuana addiction as a popular mood food.
This will depress the brains of the youth of our nation
And leave us the victims of a drugged population.

Maybe there's hope that with equal pay
Our women will feel they have now more to say.
To counteract policies based on male greed
To spending our money on the things that we need.

One thing that does help is selective immigration
Bringing in skilled people to add to our nation.
Such an influx of brains from India and China
Would give us a chance to make things go finer.

Now I think I've said quite enough
To indicate times could get tough.
What in all the world to do
I guess it'll all be left to you.

Bill Robertson 2018

We're All Canadians

It was fifty years ago I raised my hand
And learned to sing "my home and native land".
Although it was not true I sang the song
With others joined the patriotic throng.

It took not years but months to learn the truth
I'd joined a true miscellany forsooth.
With English, French, the Irish, Welsh and Scots
It was land replete with lots of plots.

And now though many years have passed away
We're really not one stable land today.
Though hosts of migrants come from many lands
We're still divided by Quebec's demands.

The French still think we're in the 14th century
With Ottawa their endless wealth dispensary.
Until they learn their just one group of many
And not deserving of an extra penny.

We're here on Earth as citizens of Canada
And not as brats demanding more from Dadda.
We welcome migrants from around the world
Marching beneath the Maple Leaf flag unfurled.

Forgetting the past we look for the times to come.
Ever together we'll march to the beat of the drum.
Always in future our family as one it must be
Close and together for us, that is always the key.

Bill Robertson 2018

Government Style and Substance

Governments world-wide and Canada too
Are strong on style in what they do.
On substance they are out to lunch
Increasingly a useless bunch.

Sometimes one will do quite well
Enjoying a favorable spell.
But mostly they are error prone
And common sense is left alone.

In truth this does not auger well
And most are on their way to hell.
Trudeau II is right on cue
And next fall will get his due.

Bill Robertson 2018

To the Milky Way

Married forty-two years to a really strange gal
And now realizing I had married an angel.
She was born far away in the Milky Way
And now she's on Earth to take me away.

I went down to find her in the desert heat
She was there with a son and a dog, it was neat.
But it took quite a while to make her go through it
As she waited for orders from H.Q. to do it.

Her name it is Sally, a Sarah at root
Her beauty was regal and attractive to boot.
Her charms overwhelmed me, I was hers from the start
I longed to be with her and never to part.

Now forty-two years on and I'm getting quite old
No longer so spritely and not quite so bold.
But I'm ready for take-off whatever the day
And soon I'll be out there in God's Milky Way.

Bill Robertson 2018

2019

Mum and Dad

Oh Dad you were always there for me, at first and last,
Fair and square, you always were both sure and fast.
All recollections I recall both clear and true,
Were such as wholly strengthened all my love for you
What is there left to say in such a joyous, blessed time
Tis only prayers of thanks to God, which are sublime.
So Dad, in heaven now receive these thoughts of mine.

Oh Mum, I know you truly loved me all my life
And didn't really like the two women who became my wives
You were too cautious to discourage on the first and bad one
And too slow to understand the second really good one.

Your cautious cry, "Oh Billy do you really think you should?"
I had to learn to ignore and decide on what was really good.
Too much discussion with you and none at all with Dad
With neither at fault, but all to do with Dad's bad Dad!

Bill Robertson 2019

Daughters Grown Older

Barbara, Christine and Marjory
All were born as daughters to me.
It happened so many years ago
But I still remember and know it was so.

Barbara came first in the year fifty-seven
A happy wee girl who was clearly God-given.
She took her first steps walking towards me
And soon she was running around full of glee.

At school she did well and came out the top girl
A Distinction she won in her study at Dal.
In Masters Studies she went her own way
Quitting and fleeing to a place no one knew.

Virtually flying out into the blue
Eventually finding a place that would do.
They say she's retired to somewhere in the West
I hope that she's happy and wish her the best.

Christine came next in the year fifty-nine
As the bigger of the twins she came first in the line.
Full of friendly emotion as she sat on my knee
It is true she always seemed happy to me.

At school she did well and especially liked Math.
In study at Toronto mainly fun was her path.
She had lots of friends, only some that I met
Then one day she called sounding full of regret.

She lived with us shortly and made a new plan
And soon a new life in investment began.
Later she met a good man of honour
And now she's married as Christine O'Connor.

Marjory came two hours after her twin
She felt that being later was a bit of a sin.
With two bigger sisters she learned to use tact
In all situations just how to react.

At school she was happy to pass all exams
And succeeded at College without any qualms.
She showed me 'lost letters' and Gran Grace's games
Which got her in trouble by that bad old dame.

When she got married to Dave with two boys
They tried to annoy me through various ploys.
That didn't work out and it's all in the past.
It's wise to be careful from first to the last.

Margie is now older and soon may retire
She has done very well and with three sons and a sire.
For as long as I live, if short or if long
Wee Margie Mole will always belong.

Bill Robertson 2019

Three Grandsons Growing

My daughter Marg she has three sons
James with Robert and Alexander.
Where they live I don't quite know
They'd have to ask their Mum to order.

James works well among the trees
And all that's there he oversees.
Before too long it's going to be
That he's in charge for all to see.

Robert too is doing well
Working where I used to dwell.
He'll be involved in large development
With varied plans he'll implement.

Alexander's studying will be supreme
And soon in time he'll be the cream.
I wish him well in his career
Which he'll pursue without a fear.

One day before my time is nigh
I hope we'll meet before we die.
And talk of things we all agree
That did us good and made us free.

Grandpa Bill Robertson 2019

Ninety Time

Now I'm coming up to ninety years of age
When the time will come to quietly turn the page.
Though it is true I do not really feel that old
I know that it is time the truth be told.

What on Earth have I been doing all these years?
Is a question that relates to my careers.
Though in work tis true my actions were quite bold
They never were rewarded much with gold.

In this life I do believe that it is best
To pursue with all one's strength a worthy quest.
Seek not rewards which give but quantity
And find the way ensuring top quality.

Bill Robertson 2019.

Sally

On a fall day in 2019
I got a message not foreseen.
"You have a problem in your rear
This may not be a happy year."

"It's cancer," Tony said for sure
I doubt if there is a valid cure.
So now it is time to do some tests
What vile disease now me infests?

They'll do some x-rays, blood tests too
Confirm diagnosis true.
Then if it is cancer they'll decide
Radiation or going inside.

So, sweetheart do not be afraid
God's Spirit comes to give us aid.
His Plan for us is all preplanned
We'll be together in the Promised Land.

Bill Robertson 2019

Sally My Darling

Oh Sally my darling, oh Sally my dear
I'm sorry I'm sick and have a sick rear.
It's time I was gone to a heavenly place
But I guess I must wait till they find me a space.

I don't feel it's fair that I'm lingering on
When most of God's angels must have advised I be gone.
Anyway right now it is what it is
So I'll just grit my teeth and take it as is.

I'm sorry that sometimes I must seem quite blunt
Cos I'm losing my words which makes me a grunt.

Bill Robertson 2019

Trudeau and Trump, A Time of Greed

I look on the world as a place of need
And find it's full of lust and greed.
I've always been blessed with enough to survive
And now, though I'm old I'm still alive.

Most of us meet some nasty souls
Attacking us to reach their goals.
They steal our lives and our careers.
One must be careful, control our fears.

Judas Iscariot did not play fair
Always taking more than his fair share.
In the end he got paid for betraying his Master
And ended his life in shameful disaster.

There are many like Judas who betray people's trust
He stole from disciples that was not just.
How many politicians steal people's money
The whole affair is not at all funny.

Donald Trump is now the lord of greed
America is back in financial lead.
Trump uses gold to gain his power,
Then power to build a golden tower.

Where else are greed-ridden powers expanding?
The Chinese Communists are everywhere demanding
And other nations seek more profit
While some don't see a way to stop it.

We're in a time of social chaos,
With many people facing loss.
It's time for governments to set up rules
To stop the world being led by fools.

I believe that God must have a wife.
It's time she moved to stop the strife.
While men create a global mess
Women's wisdom will impress.

It's time that women take the lead
The world is in a state of need.
Trump's wife Melanja is a Slovene
She could be a wisdom Queen!

If that's too much to contemplate
Maybe we'll have to sit and wait.
Who knows it's time to take a break
And have a piece of Christmas cake!

Bill Robertson 2019

The Start of the Slump

The US and Canada are on their way down
It's sad but true they are losing their crown.
As usual it's Canada taking the brunt
We respond all together with hardly a grunt.

With a Trudeau in power for another four years
It's enough to bring Canadians to bitter tears.
Those who voted him back will learn their mistake
As they watch French Quebec get another big take.

Four more years of Trudeau will really give them a chance
To gain more power and plan more advance.
With the Rest of Canada snoozing in a heavy dream sleep
Quebeckers as usual will take another big leap.

The next choice will be to join a French Quebec state
Or go begging to Trump to make us another US state.
And that will be the end of the Canada we love
When that time comes, Oh God please take me "above".

Bill Robertson 2019

www.ingramcontent.com/pod-product-compliance
Lightning Source LLC
Chambersburg PA
CBHW081234090426
42738CB00016B/3300